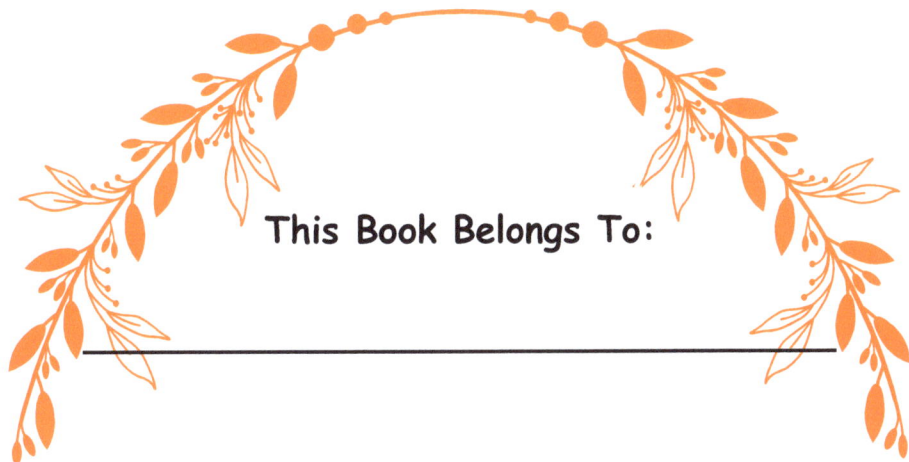

This Book Belongs To:

_____

Presented By:

On:

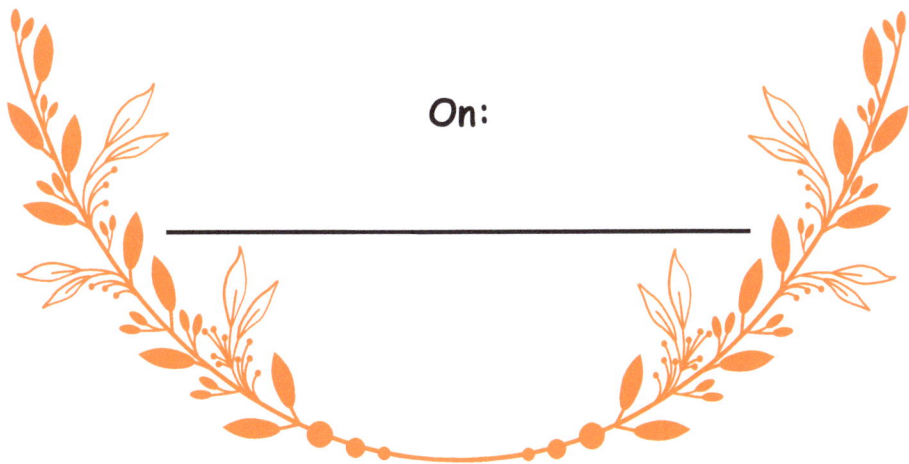

I dedicate this book to my mom and dad,
James and Anna.
Yours was one of the best love stories.
Thanks for being great parents.

First hardback edition August 2024

Janice Millane Wasmer also authored the first book in this series, "In God's Creation Animals of the Forest."

Book design by Janice Millane Wasmer WildArtAmerica Publishing.
Special thanks and appreciation to my two editor-daughters,
Janelle L. Channell and Renaya G. Van Dusen.
Without their loving support, encouragement, and editing this book for me, this endeavor would have been much more difficult.
Furthermore, I would like to thank my husband, Ed Wasmer, who supports me and my art in every human way possible. To him, I am most grateful.

ISBN 979-8-9907327-0-4 Hardback

www.janicemillanewasmer.com

In God's Creation

Animals of the Desert

A Book for "Kids" of All Ages

Written and Illustrated by Janice Millane Wasmer

I had such a tremendous learning experience when I wrote and illustrated my first book, "In God's Creation Animals of the Forest," that I immediately started this second book. Wow!

I've always admired my mom. She gave birth to 11 children. I could stop right there as enough reason to admire her, but she was so much more. She always had a positive attitude about her. I seriously do not remember my mom ever being negative. When I was in my teens and prone to feeling sorry for myself, my mom's advice was always, "Just do something for someone else. It will get you out of that funk quickly!" If I followed this wise advice, it worked every time. Another thing about Mom is that she wanted to write a book about her life. Before she passed at the good old age of 92, she did manage to write a story, but it was only given to family members. It never became a published book. After experiencing raising 11 children, I'm sure it would have been a best seller. I owe my "Momma" so much. She always encouraged my creativity and would somehow purchase all the art materials I thought I needed. She also liked to enter me into all those little art contests that would appear in magazines back in the day. I think of my mom often and know I will see her again one day. I wish she could have been here to see all I've done in the later years of my life. I can be comforted, though, because, you know, she probably does see me.

"Trust the Lord with all your heart.
Don't depend on your own understanding.
Remember the Lord in everything you do.
And he will give you success." Proverbs 3:5-6

In God's Creation
Animals of the Desert
A Book for "Kids" of All Ages

"The heavens tell the glory of God.
And the skies announce what his hands have made."
Psalm 19:1

Deep in the desert, in God's great creation, many creatures live. From the smallest scary scorpion to the desert cougar, they each have their place and their purpose. God loves them all and will forever provide them abundant food, fresh water, and crispy, clean air. He watches over them with His love and His care.

"The wild animals in the fields will thank me, the jackals and owls, too, for giving them water in the desert." Isaiah 43:20 (NLT)

Tracing the eerie paths left by scuttling scorpions in the scorching desert unveils a hidden world of fun and quirky critters. They somehow stay alive in this dry and arid place. But even here, God provides for them. No one knows why a scorpion will shine brightly when seen under a black light. But God indeed does! Scouting for scorpions at night with a black light is really fun to do. But don't fear a scorpion because they are more afraid of you!

"You fathers—if your children ask for a fish, do you give them a snake instead? Or if they ask for an egg, do you give them a scorpion? Of course not!"   Luke 11:11-12

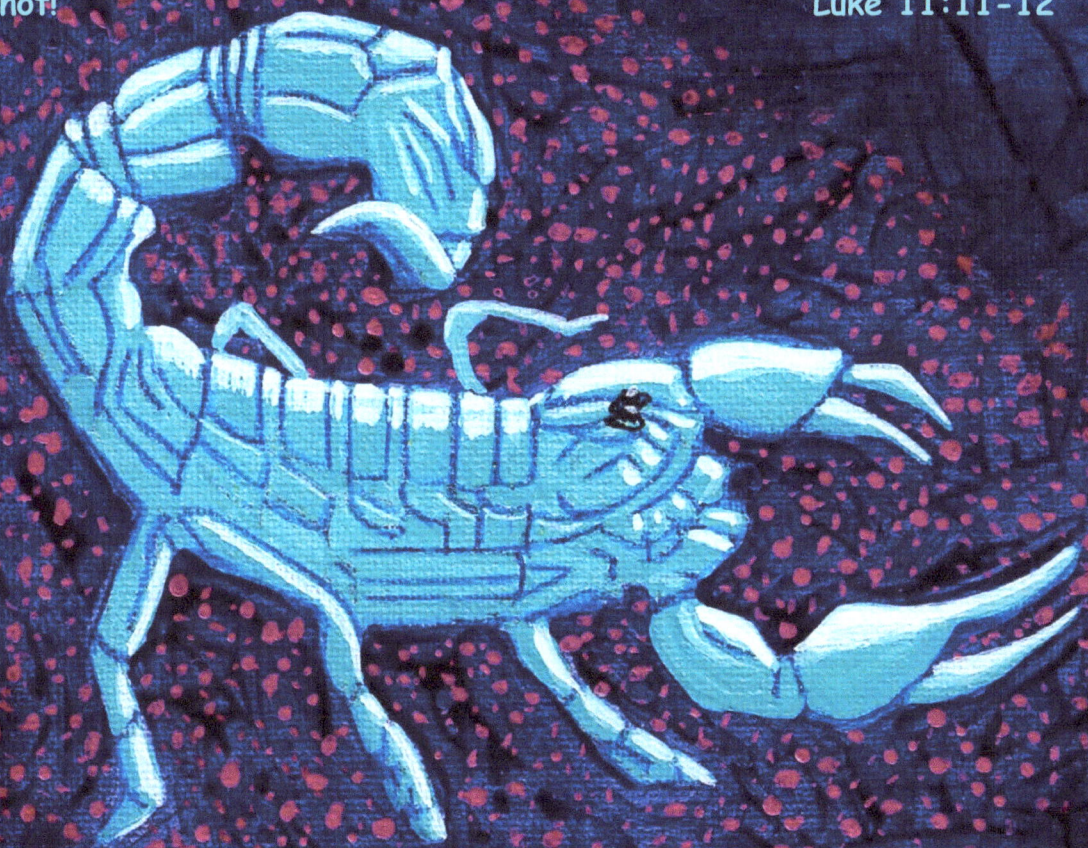

"You might find a bird's nest by the road. It might be in a tree or on the ground. And the mother bird might be sitting on the young birds or eggs. Do not take the mother bird with the young birds."
Deuteronomy 22:6

In God's **beautiful** creation, in the quiet of the morning, the first bird you may hear is a Gambel's quail calling. The topknot on their heads bob as they roam free, with their plump little bodies as cute as can be. Their eggs are hidden in nests on the ground, and Mommy talking to them before hatching is the sweetest little sound.

"Then God Said, "Let the water be filled with living things. And let birds fly in the air above the earth."
Genesis 1:20

In God's glorious creation, something "takes the cake." Do you know that roadrunners eat rattlesnakes? He can dart through cactus, rocks, and sand, up to 25 miles per hour, at speeds so grand. It makes a sound so sharp and clear. That's called a buzz, a coo, or a whirr. This bird runs in rapid flight. It races the desert both day and night.

"Now the snake was the most cleaver of all the wild animals the Lord God had made. One day the snake spoke to the woman. He said 'Did God really say that you must not eat fruit from any tree in the garden?'" Genesis 3:1

In God's wonderful creation lives one sidewinder, also known as "Horned"; the scales above its eyes make it look all scorned. In the vast desert so swiftly it slides, with a wiggle it likes to glide. Fastest moving of all snakes, with its tail it likes to fake. It lures its prey so cunningly, blending in the desert so stunningly. With its rattle and with a shake, it claims, "Beware, I'm a rattlesnake!"

"'Wolves and lambs will eat together in peace. Lions will eat hay like oxen. A snake on the ground will not hurt anyone. They will not hurt or destroy each other on all my holy mountain,' says the Lord."
Isaiah 65:25

In God's awesome creation, deep in the desert, so hot and bright, lives the stealthy cougar out of human sight. Only eating once a week keeps her slender, quick, and sleek. She hides her meal that she can't finish, keeping her body oh so thinnish. She hunts her food on a quiet, cool night and sleeps all day until moonlight. She leaps and she bounds with silent grace, leaving paw prints all over the place!

"He makes us more clever than the animals of the earth. He makes us wiser than the birds of the air." Job 35:11

In God's creative creation in the desert, warm and dry, lives one silly cactus wren who doesn't love to fly. Its plumage is brown, with black and white spots all around. You will find him mainly on the ground. He chooses his partner once and for life, with a chirp like an engine instead of a fife. He builds his nest in prickly places, with a cozy spot in hidden spaces. The largest of wrens, this is one big bird! He may be pretty, but he's no songbird.

"The burning desert will have pools of water. The dry ground will have springs. Where wild dogs once lived, grass and water plants will grow." Isaiah 35:7

In God's incredible creation, where the sun blazes high, roams the desert coyote beneath the endless sky. He doesn't just howl but yelps and barks. He's out on the prowl until late after dark. An omnivore, consuming both plants and meat. He is a survivor and not fussy about what he eats. Mom and Dad are good parents; they share, raising their young with sweet, tender care.

"Tell the people of Jerusalem, 'Your king is coming to you. He is gentle and riding on a donkey. He is on the colt of a donkey.'"
Matthew 21:5

In God's magnificent creation with ears so long, a stubborn little burro grazes daylong. Highly intelligent and stubborn as can be, she roams the desert wild and free. If you see a burro in the wild, remember she's a desert child. With friends like coyote, the lizard, and the hare, she finds adventure everywhere.

"Jesus said to him, 'The foxes have holes to live in. The birds have nests to live in. But the Son of Man has no place where he can rest his head.'" Matthew 8:20

In God's immense creation with fur gold as wheat, the kit fox's large ears are for hearing and releasing heat. Darting through bushes and leaping over rocks, clever and cunning, is this little fox. He digs his home in burrows in the ground, where he sleeps, all cozy, safe, and sound. He travels in groups called "skulk" or "leash" under the sky so bright, prowling the sands both day and night.

"The desert and dry land will become happy. The desert will be glad and will produce flowers. Like a flower, it will have many blooms. It will show its happiness, as if it is shouting with joy. It will be beautiful like the forest of Lebanon. It will be as beautiful as the hill of Carmel and the Plain of Sharon. All people will see the glory of the Lord. They will see the splendor of our God." Isaiah 35:1-2

In God's amazing creation, the most giant rabbit, though quick and light, moves so easily out of sight. He moves like an antelope as he dodges prey. This silly rabbit runs swiftly away. His ears are long, furry, and sleek, and the antelope jackrabbit is quite unique. By day, he rests in shady spots; by night, he hops and hops and hops. I think he may never stop!

"I will make rivers flow on the dry hills. I will make springs of water flow through the valleys. I will change the desert into a lake of water. I will change the dry land into springs of water."
Isaiah 41:18

In God's bountiful creation in the desert, dry and wide, the desert tortoise slowly strides. Its hardened shell, which is rigid and round, protects this creature as it moves on the ground. It digs burrows cool and deep, collecting fresh water to keep. The desert tortoise can go a whole year without drinking water but do not fear. This remarkable creature, which is rarely seen, munches on cactus so moist and green.

"So God made the wild animals, the tame animals and all the small crawling animals to produce more of their own kind. God saw that this was good." Genesis 1:25

In God's stunning creation, woodrat scurries, building its nest with fluff, twigs, and flurries and gathering treasures by day and by night, whiskers twitching. Oh, what a sight! She munches on desert plants while dancing with a bit of prance. A tiny builder, fast but neat, making desert life so sweet.

"I have given all the green plants to all the animals to eat. They will be food for every wild animal, every bird of the air and every small crawling animal. And it happened." Genesis 1:30

In God's beloved creation, with tremendous speed, he moves through sand dunes and prickly weeds. The antelope squirrel darts and dashes. With his tail held high, he dances and prances. He gathers seeds and nuts to eat and finds shady spots to escape the heat. A tiny creature in the desert land, oh how he loves the desert sand.

"Praise him, you wild animals and all cattle, small crawling animals and birds." Psalm 148:10

In God's marvelous creation, a stealthy Gila monster with careful grace has a silly smile on her scaly face. With a flick of her tongue, she tastes the air, looking wild with a hardened stare. She loves munching eggs and bugs and will even eat slimy slugs. She's so happy in her desert home; she can rest, play, dance, and roam. With colorful scales of black, red, and white, a "bit scary," she comes out at night.

"Everything the Lord does is right. With love he takes care of all he has made." Psalm 145:17

In God's brilliant creation in the desert, hot and bright, lives a zebra-tailed lizard on his toes, quick and light. When danger comes, he runs so fast. In the race, he sprints so he won't be last. He waves his tail to distract his foe, and into the sand, low he will go. This lizard is so pretty, with bright colors on his tummy, but eating bugs and flies is, to us, not so yummy.

"But Jesus called the little children to him and said to his followers, 'Let the little children come to me. Don't stop them, because the kingdom of God belongs to people who are like these little children.'" Luke 18:16

In God's excellent creation, with bristly dark fur and a collar of white, lives the great javelina, who is solid but slight. A peccary, not a pig, but for some strange reason, they don't grow as big. A smelly scent gland on the top of their rump marks their territory on a tree or a stump. In family groups, they are known to stay; they stick together and will not stray. Their babies can be born yearlong, called "reds." In caves and under trees, Mommy puts them to bed.

"The Lord is good to everyone. He is merciful to all he has made. Lord, everything you have made will praise you. Those who belong to you will bless you." Psalm 145:9-10

In God's majestic creation, a ringtail cat has eyes so big and ears upright, which helps her as she prowls at night. Early settlers and miners kept her as a pet, so she is called a "miner's cat." A member of the raccoon family, she hunts the desert gleefully. So if you see this masked face, remember she holds a special place. In the desert, she has the title of the Arizona state mammal. Her tail has rings that are black and white, which cleverly give her foes a fright. A ringtail cat, so small and clever, will roam the desert forever and ever.

"I am like a desert owl. I am like an owl living among the ruins."
Psalm 102:6

In God's powerful creation, a tiny elf owl makes her nest. In a woodpecker hole in a saguaro, she'll rest. Though tiny, she is bold and brave, facing the night in her quaint little "cave." She hoots a small cry, not loud but clear, telling all, "I'm hunting here!" With a wingspan short, she flits through the air, catching moths and flying insects without any care.

"The Lord's love never ends.
His mercies never stop.
They are new every morning.
Lord, your loyalty is great."
Lamentations 3:22-23

In God's astounding creation is a horned lizard called "toad," it crawls on its belly and is quite bold. It likes to eat ants, its favorite treat. With the flick of its tongue, it is certainly neat. With spikes on its back and horns on its head, the sandy desert it calls its bed. When predators threaten, it has a neat trick, it puffs up its body to make itself thick. It sometimes squirts blood out of its eyes, which its predators find a scary surprise.

"So know that the Lord your God is God. He is the faithful God. He will keep his agreement of love for a thousand lifetimes. He does this for people who love him and obey his commands."
Deuteronomy 7:9

In God's splendorous creation, the great horned owl is the mightiest of all. His haunting hoot is his recognized call. A hoot that's clear and echoes wide in the desert countryside. With a beak so strong and talons keen, he catches his prey sight unseen. He is the master of the night. He is so wise and proud. The great horned owl stands out in the crowd.

"He taught about many different kinds of plants. He taught about everything from the great cedar trees of Lebanon to the hyssop that grows out of the walls. He also taught about animals, birds, crawling things and fish." 1 Kings 4:33

In God's blessed creation lives a little creepy crawly. She has a hairy, scary body. While creeping through the night, finding places to hide in the big open desert, deep and wide. The tarantula spins no web to catch her prey; she hunts on the ground in her own special way. With fangs so sharp but venom mild, she captures her food, fierce and wild. If she is threatened, she raises her legs high to scare off predators as they pass by.

In God's divine creation, He always has a plan. He has loved all of His creatures since the world began. He made us in His image; creating is His specialty. On this earth that He made, He blesses all humanity. This story is ending, but this you must know. God is our creator, and He loves us all so. His love is eternal, and He purposed to send His Son to forgive us forever to the end. So please accept that His gift of forgiveness is completed. Because your enemy satan is once and for all defeated. Jesus Christ, your Redeemer is always by your side. He promised to be near you and always be your guide. You have a purpose on this earth, and may His glory be in you forever. May His blessings be on you and your household without measure.

"For this is how God loved the world: He gave his one and only Son, so that everyone who believes in him will not perish but have eternal life." John 3:16

It's not over yet!

www.ingramcontent.com/pod-product-compliance
Lightning Source LLC
Chambersburg PA
CBHW041548260326
41914CB00016B/1584